Why God Chose Me

*Thanks for your support.
Be blessed.
Monique L Rhe*

Why God Chose Me

✦

"Monique L. Rhea's Journey thru Molestation, Rocky Relationships, Diabetes, Death and Cancer"

Monique L. Rhea

iUniverse, Inc.

New York Lincoln Shanghai

Why God Chose Me
"Monique L. Rhea's Journey thru Molestation, Rocky Relationships, Diabetes, Death and Cancer"

iUniverse books may be ordered through booksellers or by contacting:

iUniverse
2021 Pine Lake Road, Suite 100
Lincoln, NE 68512
www.iuniverse.com
1-800-Authors (1-800-288-4677)

ISBN: 978-0-595-47966-5 (pbk)
ISBN: 978-0-595-60064-9 (ebk)

Printed in the United States of America

This book is dedicated to a team of supporters. Without them, my journey would have been impossible.

To my soul mate, Matthew Dilworth—thank you for being there with me through thick and thin and looking beyond my faults and personal emotions. You are truly God-sent, I love you more than words could ever express. I look forward to the journey God has destined for our lives.

To my parents, John L. and Terri V. Rhea—words could never express how I truly feel. I thank God for your love, your support, your kind hearts, your wisdom, your love for your family and most importantly, your love for God. If I would ask for another set of parents, I could only ask that they be in the image of you both!! Thank you for always being there through the good, bad and rough times. I know sometimes as children, we do not always show just how dear our parents are to us. But, without you, I would not be in the mind set that I am today. You have been such an inspiration to my life and have groomed me to be what I am today.

To my son, DaQuan T. Dilworth—thank you for being you and allowing God to use you in ways you can not imagine. Thanks for loving me regardless of the situation or circumstance. You are truly an angel and a blessing sent from above. I thank God for allowing me to bring you into this world. I love you unconditionally.

To my daughters, Veronica A. Pope, Miesha L. Brown and Meia M. Brown—Veronica and Miesha, even though I did not give birth to the two of you, I thank you for allowing me to enter into your lives and sharing your lives with me. Meia, with Matt and me not being your parents, I want you to know that you were truly God sent. I did not birth three daughters into this world, but I have gained three daughters into my life. I love you unconditionally.

To my siblings, Renell and Ottawa Rhea, Myron Dilworth and Melanie Ragland—thank you for the love that you show and the support that is always provided. My parents only gave birth to two (Renell and myself); however, I have gained two sisters and another brother. The words in-law and play sister are not in our vocabulary that we use in describing family. I love you much.

To my other family and friends—thank you for all the love and support you have shown and for being an instrumental force in my life during these times.

But most importantly, I thank God, Who allowed and enabled me to go through these life challenges victoriously.

Contents

Acknowledgements

While going through certain situations in your life, it is evident that God has placed people there for a reason. Knowing that they were God sent is truly uplifting and an inspiration. I would like to acknowledge the following for allowing God to be instrumental in their lives, acknowledging Him in it all and helping me along my journey.

Aesthetica Chicago, LLC—Dr. Roxanne Sylora and staff.
Metro Center for Health—Dr. Deborah Basile
Pronger Smith Medical Center—Dr. Refat Baridi and the oncology staff, Dr. Ramon Manglano and Dr. Esmond Yen
Southern Cook Radiation Oncology—Dr Gregorio Tolentino and staff.
Third Baptist Church of Chicago—Rev. Dr. Alan V. Ragland, Pastor

Introduction

In January of 1973 at 8:27 p.m., Monique was born into the world. She was new life in this world, but did not know what life had to offer or what was destined for her life. But God knew from inception, the path that He would have her to follow and the ways He would have her to go. From the beginning, she has always been outspoken and one who would speak her mind. She was destined to be in this world. By the age of two months, she was featured in the April 5, 1973 issue of the Jet Magazine, along with Rev. Elmer Fowler (pastor and founder of Third Baptist Church of Chicago) and Mrs. Pearl Brown. Mrs. Brown (age 91) and Monique were highlighted as the youngest and oldest members of Third Baptist Church.

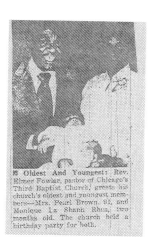

■ Oldest And Youngest: Rev. Elmer Fowler, pastor of Chicago's Third Baptist Church, greets his church's oldest and youngest members—Mrs. Pearl Brown, 91, and Monique La Shann Rhea, two months old. The church held a birthday party for both.

This was God's way of introducing her into the world and let the world know that a survivor was on the way and letting the devil know that he would have his hands full with this Child of God. Whatever he had coming her way, God was going to be in the midst of it all and that no weapon formed against her shall prosper. Look out devil; you want a fight you are going to get one!!! God had strapped on her armor the day she was born. He knew what she needed in the life He had planned and destined.

Have you ever wondered why you were born or why so many trials and tribulations happen in your life? For years, Monique has thought and questioned the same thing, "What was her purpose in life?" She felt that no one understood her feelings or the pain she was experiencing in life. Monique felt as if God had forgotten her. She pondered quite often as to why must one so young be faced with so many challenges and still have so much to live for. God felt His child's pain and decided to turn what Monique felt was a misery into a ministry. He spoke clearly to her and affirmed that she needed to express her emotions and let the world know why she was chosen and how she made it through. With this, God has given her so many answers to life questions and boldly identified her purpose. This is why she had to share her experiences with the world. She knows that she is *not alone* and others *need* to hear her story and to let them know that they are not alone as well. So sit back and open your mind into the life experiences of Monique L. Rhea.

1

The Downfalls Begin

Unfortunately, my childhood is much of a blur with the exception of a few tragedies that I can remember. I take that back, a few life learning experiences. I believe my childhood was such a blur because I tried to block so many things from my memory. By not remembering I would feel as if none of it happened. My Dad and Mom have always been opened-minded and honest with my brother and me. At a very young age, they talked about life, sex, moral ethics and right and wrong. I could have never asked for better parents; however, even though they were open, I still kept things hidden from them. By the age of nine, early woman-hood began to kick in. I started my menstrual period as well as developed breast. In the beginning, this was exciting because it was as if I was maturing into a young woman, plus I had one up on all my other female cousins.

However, by the age of ten, I really did not like this maturing thing. I found that I was beginning to be noticed and others looked at me in a way that I was uncomfortable with. Things began to happen to me that a ten year old should not have experienced—I was fondled, molested. My molester was four years older than me and knew what he was doing. He touched me in spots that were sacred and made me touch him in ways that made me feel uncomfortable. At the time, I did not know whether I should like the feelings I was feeling or should I be disgusted. I knew this was wrong and truly felt violated. I felt as if something was being taken away from me, like a dark cloud began to surface over me. I did not want to talk about it because I did not want anyone to get into trouble or be punished. And most importantly, I felt as if I would be looked upon as one who lied or exaggerated the truth. I learned later that hurt people, hurt people and that this was also happening to him. But regardless of the fact, it was wrong! From that day forward, I began to shut down emotionally and my life was no longer my own. I allowed the molestation and its effect take over and get the best of me.

As I grew, my parents who were very loving and affectionate detected a difference in my attitude, my self esteem and my appearance. They would constantly approach me and ask me if everything was okay and if there was anything I needed to talk to them about. Time after time, I would deny that anything was wrong and would reply that I was fine. Their constant questioning began to aggravate me. I guess because they knew me too well. They still suspected that something was going on, but I refused to talk. Looking back, I know this response was normal of an undeserving victim. It appears that we, as young ladies, often take abuse in some weird way as our responsibility for the actions that were brought upon us. I was a young girl entrapped in a woman's body. I was developing breast, menstruating and changing overall in my body. Though I had no control, I felt it must have been my fault. Shortly after this time, I began to have frequent nightmares about a man coming after me. But I never saw the face of this predator. I was afraid to go to sleep. Life seemed to be so complicated at such a young age. However, little did I know that my journey was just beginning.

Of course, by the age of eleven or twelve, I really started to notice the boys in my class, but they seem so much older than me. This was due to my double in the fourth grade. Always being on the big-girl side growing up, boys were not noticing me as much as I was noticing them. My self esteem and inner self began to crumble. No longer was I feeling beautiful inside or outside. I hated myself and the way I was. I blamed myself for all that was happening in my life. "It was all my fault; I am getting what I deserved"!

2

The Cover Up

Entering high school was the most exciting time of my life. I felt very important entering as a freshman as I knew a lot of people. This was because my older cousins, who attended the same school, introduced me to the upper classmen. So I did not come in as a typical Freshie. I was known and it felt good—I was noticed and accepted. As you can see, I began to seek approval from others. While in high school, although excited, I began to lose myself—I began to lose Monique. By the age of 15, my sophomore year, I thought I was in love and no one could tell me differently. There was a guy, let's call him Vick, which I was head-over-heels for. But he thought he was God's gift to women. At that time, I felt like I was the luckiest girl in the whole world because he was with me! He told me all that a girl with low self-esteem wanted to hear. For example, some of the lines he would use was, "I love you", "There's no one else in the world for me but you", "We have something special", "I'm yours and only yours" and the list goes on. But little did I know that all these sweet nothings were told to only have victory over what was most precious, my virginity. Although the sex was consensual, I felt violated once again. I was not ready for this adult act emotionally. However, even though receiving suggestions from my older girl cousins to wait, I thought I had to give in to be loved and accepted. A few months later, we broke up because "*he felt he needed some space"*. Yeah, right!! The truth was that he was moving on to the next victim!

I had other boyfriends after this but nothing serious. My junior year of high school, here I go again thinking and saying, *"I'm in luv"* with someone who also attended my school, let's call him Stan. Stan was not the most popular at the time, but he treated me like I wanted to be treated. He visited frequently, gave me gifts and took me out occasionally. These were things I was not use to. After graduating from high school, to me it seemed everything was fine. We made the choice of attending the same college. In the beginning this was great. But as I look back, I can tell you this was not a smart decision.

On the first day of being away, my so-called love cheated on me. He arrived at school a day before I did and it seemed he got very acquainted with the opposite sex quickly. I was not on campus one hour before the rumors begin to spread of him being with another girl. I confronted him and he admitted to his actions. With my self-esteem being so low at the time, I excused it, forgave him and we continued to date. I thought things were going well and were back on track. We dated until the second semester of our first year. I helped him when he was pledging a Frat and even attended his Frat Ball. But to my surprise, his wondering eyes had a Soro Sister already in line. Within a few weeks after the ball, he decided that he needed a break. A month after our break-up, he started dating this Soro Sister. I was devastated and torn to pieces. I do not know how I made it through the last two semesters of college. Being home-sick, heart-broken, and to top it off worrying how my parents were going to be able to continue to pay for my education, I left school. I had the opportunity of going back to a job I had during high school. So I took the job. Though we went our separate ways, I still saw him occasionally during the summer and even dropped him off at his new fiancé's house. Oh, by the way, I forgot to mention that after about two or three months of him dating his Soro Sister, he got engaged! How naïve was I!

I was very vulnerable and anyone saying the right thing, showing a little attention, pretending that they cared, would really sweep me off my feet. I dated other guys, but no one filled that void.

I ran into Vick again soon after starting the job. It was like the world was new and I fell in love all over again. Believe me, it was not love, but I was afraid of being alone. We started to date again and he swore that it would be different this time. In the beginning, it was great and things were going well! However, an inner voice began to speak to me, saying, "He's a Dog, move on", but did I listen? No! I started getting annoying telephone calls on my private line from other individuals who would not speak when I answered the phone. There were strange numbers on my pager that Vick called me from. He would take my car and not bring it back until the next morning. I missed several days of work because of him. My parents had even seen him in my car with other females. But because I was so head over heels in love with him, if they told me I think it would have pushed me just that much closer to him. So they decided not to tell me, and I am glad they did not. I had to learn the hard way. I was blinded by this so-called love, and began to grow bitter with this relationship. Instead of walking away, I decided to get even.

3

From Darkness To Light

I met a guy name Matthew who was different from all of the rest of the guys I dated in the past. He was also a friend of Vick's and a close friend to my cousin, Candy. As we hung out, we became more acquainted with each other. We actually met my junior year of high school and our relationship was strictly platonic. I guess when I saw him a few years earlier, he did not seem the same to me. But this time, was totally different, he truly caught my eye. Hanging out with him seemed different, it was fun and genuine. He was not interested in me buying him things or driving my car or wanting any money from me. These were things I had done in the past to keep a man. I started to get a realization of how a true friend and relationship should be. Although, I was trying to relax and trust, I still kept up my guard, waiting for the next betrayal by a male. But, we really enjoyed each other's company, so I decided to relax a little.

Even though I said in my mind and felt in my heart that this relationship was only to get revenge on Vick, our platonic relationship blossomed into a daily must-see-him. I would park my car in the alley behind Matt's house. As you see, Vick lived across the street with his mother and I did not want to be caught. Vick decided to go off to college, so I took this as a perfect time for Matt and I to get even closer. However, Vick's mother would see me from time to time so I would still hide my car. There were times when I would be unaware of Vick's pop-up visits. Matthew and I would be driving down the street, upon noticing him; we would back-up and go the opposite way. Strange as it seems, I did not want to be caught even though I no longer had feelings for Vick. My feelings grew stronger for Matt and I knew some family members would not approve of our relationship. I believe it was because Matt was not the type of guy I normally dated. He was more streetwise than the average school boy type I have dated in the past. For me, it was about making my family happy, not just my Mom and Dad, but the entire family. Trying to satisfy them instead of doing what was right for me. So I continued to sneak in seeing Matt. However, one day, Matt's mother approached me and said, "If you have feelings for my son, you need to stop hiding. You need to let the other guy know that you do not want to be with him any longer. He's a dog, he hurt you, now move on!!" (This is written very mildly as Mama Ora had some really choice words).

So I decided to do just that, while visiting Matt, this time I parked my car in the front of the house. This was the day that Vick was home from school and saw my vehicle there. The doorbell rang; Matt and I were in his room watching TV. Mama Ora opened the door, it was Vick. She invited him in and told him Matt was in his room. She thought that was hilarious. So of course, when he sees me lying on the bed, his mouth flew open. He was in complete shock and could not believe what he was seeing. But at that moment and time, I felt good because at last I got even!!! "Finally got you back, now you know how it feels". Vick left upset, but harassed us all night long by knocking on the window, but we ignored him. That night he left and I guess went home. All we knew was that we were at peace for the night.

Vick tried to aggravate and disturb my new relationship by playing games. While visiting Matt another time, when leaving I noticed that my car had been moved. My car was parked across the street instead of in front of the house where I had parked it. Could it be that an additional set of car keys were made by Vick? Matt said enough was enough and finally confronted Vick. He told Vick he had to move on because our relationship was getting serious.

During this time in my life, alcohol and marijuana began to play an active role. I was grown, it was my life, and I can do what I want to do. As hanging-out buddies, it was okay for me to drink and smoke with him. However, Matt was very much against me using either of these non-"lady-like" influences now that we were an item. I had a hard time understanding this; as it was okay previously, why not now? There are some personal reasons why he felt so harshly. He had first-hand knowledge of what drugs and alcohol can do and how they can destroy the best of families.

As mentioned earlier, my relationship with Matt would not have the family stamp of approval. You see, he had his own car and owned a lot of jewelry. Assumptions were being made that he had to be doing something illegal, but all of these items were received at the passing of his father at the age of seventeen. Matt was a radical type of person. He had no problem in expressing his feelings and letting others know when to mind their own business. Matt would not allow others to enter into his space without his approval. He was known for voicing his opinion and demanding his respect. Matt was by far no angel as he had done things that society today has categorized our young black males as doing, selling drugs. Was he proud of it? No, he was not!! But he did what he felt he had to do, he had responsibilities at a young age. You see, when Matt and I met, he had already had a seven month old daughter named Veronica, of which he had at the age of seventeen. Veronica would be around all the time, I would play with her as she was such a special sweet child.

4

The Blessing Arrives

As we continued to date, every now and then, things got a little rocky for us because of my fears and expectations of being hurt again. I would purposely start an argument or I would do things to stay away a couple of days just to get a break. I could feel myself falling deep and feeling the closeness. So pushing back was my defense to detach myself. However, on February 22, 1993, I began to get really bad stomach cramps. My parents rushed me to the hospital and my father being who he is, looked back and stated that he knew what was wrong with me, "Yo butt is pregnant". I am crying and saying, "No Daddy, I'm not. I went to the doctor previously and he stated that I had gotten a pelvic infection and had prescribed some medicine to take." (I did not tell my Dad that an inner voice told me not to take the pills of which I did not) We are now in the Emergency Room and I am in a room by myself. Being nineteen years of age, I did not require a parent's presence, so they waited for me in the Waiting Room.

While waiting for the test results, the attending physician asked if I was pregnant. I told him no and advised him of my previous doctor's visit and diagnosis. But when the test results came back, they read otherwise. I cried and truly bawled, because I thought that I was going to be the biggest disappointment to my parents. Here it is, they are doing everything they can to raise me the right way and do everything possible for me, and I become pregnant! What am I to do, what is it that I can say? I looked at the doctor and asked him to call my mother in. When she walked in the room and saw my face, she knew instantly that I was pregnant. All I could do is hug her and tell her that I was sorry. I was sorry for disappointing her and sorry for getting pregnant. But, being the Mom that she is, she just hugged me and told me that it will be okay.

On the same day, I was taken for an ultrasound, but upon review, they could not see the baby, so they thought I was pregnant in my tubes. I was terrified and did not know what was happening or where all this was going to lead. They decided to send me up to surgery for a laparoscopy. I called Matt before I went up to surgery to let him know that I was indeed pregnant and they wanted to verify if the baby was in my tubes. Because of all of the games that I played and all the things that were going on in our relationship, he was in disbelief. He thought that I was lying to him again. It was not until he looked at the caller I.D. and noted the call was made from the hospital that he believed otherwise. As it turned out, the baby was just too small to see and not visible on the ultrasound. Now it is evident that not only was I "destined" to be in this world but my son was as well.

Upon my release, Matt had come to the hospital to drive me home. All the way home, we did not exchange any words; we just stared occasionally at one another. Entering my house, my Dad was sitting in the kitchen after a hard day of work. I think Matt was a little afraid to come in as he did not know what my Dad was going to say or do. My Dad looked at both of us and asked, "What are your intentions about the pregnancy." We both said that we were going to keep and raise the baby. I personally did not believe in abortions, so that thought never entered my mind. This was my first and only time that I ever became pregnant.

When I went to my attending physician during my first trimester he continually had negative comments. I should have known then to change doctors, but I did not. Some of his exact words to me were "Don't be too excited about being pregnant, you may end up miscarrying anyway because the baby is too little:" I was devastated and hurt by his remarks and lack of compassion. Because of this, I was overly cautious about everything that I did in an effort not to cause a miscarriage. It was hard trying to maintain caution. I was enrolled in a Cosmetology School which required standing for long periods of time. So needless to say, I was under stress from education, employment, and trying to keep my baby safe.

By my fifth month of pregnancy, I told Matt that I just knew I was having a boy, a son for him. Our relationship was continually going well and growing. Matt began to scare me as he started talking about settling down and becoming a family. He would state "Let's go somewhere where it's just us, no distractions. Let's start a new beginning. Let's move to a place where we would have only us to rely on so that we can become a close family unit." Hearing him talk like this made my danger flag go up. I had become overwhelmed and things were moving too fast. I did not know what to do. So I reverted back to what I knew, pushing away, both physically and emotionally. But Matt still cared and wanted to be around especially since I was carrying his son. Things were getting a little rocky due to my attempt to disconnect. We were just going along, merely surviving.

Around my eight month of pregnancy, with all of the stress, confusion, emotional distress, as well as the physical pain I was experiencing, I went to see my OB/GYN doctor. I advised him that I was tired, not feeling well and asked about departure from work. However, this is the same doctor that told me not to be overly excited about my pregnancy. He said that I was just being lazy and being twenty years old, I should be grateful that I have a job and I should take myself to work. He also stated that back in the day, women did not have such opportunities and privileges. He was the *BIGGEST*

JERK there was; he should not have been given a license to practice in a field where he assisted bringing life into the world. It took a lot of effort but I had finally received a release from work from my primary care physician.

One week had passed and early one morning I began getting some very bad cramps. It seemed they were coming quite often, about every five minutes or so. I called OB/GYN's office to advise them. My Mom began to get so excited because her grandbaby was coming! We called my doctor and Dr. "Jerk" told me that there was no way that the contractions were that strong, the baby was not due yet, and I still had about three weeks to go. But, even from the beginning, I believe I knew the due date and that his date was wrong. Because I was enrolled under an HMO Plan, I had to listen to the attending physician. Dr. "Jerk", said to wait for the contractions to get stronger and closer together". I called him shortly after advising him of an update, he then tells me to go the hospital.

By the time that I got to the emergency room that day, I had already dilated to three centimeters and the pain was getting stronger and stronger. Support was present. Along with Matt, were my parents and my two cheerleading cousins, Candy and Dionne. They had been planning to make sure they were there for the birth. They kept trying to make me laugh and keep my mind off of the pain. They kept saying things like, "Does it hurt? Boy, you know your breath sure does stink, you need a mint!!" Only one person could be in the delivery room at a time, so after Matt visited for a while he went home to shower and change clothes as he was just getting off of work. Finally, on October 8, 1993, at 10:27 p.m., weighing seven pounds, ten ounces, our son was born into the world. We had always talked about naming the baby a junior. Matt had tried to revisit that evening, but because of his height and his youthful face, the hospital would not let him up to visit, even though he had identification. He was told that it was after visiting hours. So he went home disgusted and disappointed.

I had called him the next morning to advise him that the hospital was coming around to obtain signatures for the birth certificate. The hospital indicated that unless the father was present at the hospital, a baby could not be named a junior, as the father's consent was a requirement. I had tried calling to verify the whereabouts of Matt and to find out how soon he would arrive. I found out that he should be arriving shortly. When the hospital representative came to my room, Matt had not yet arrived and the representative would not wait. I wanted my son to have a name, so I called him DaQuan Terrell Rhea. Within the hour, Matt finally arrived. He looked excited and had a proud look on his face. He picked him up tenderly and noticed the name tag on the baby's bed. It read Rhea instead of Dilworth. He looked so hurt and expressed that he felt betrayed. Needless to say, that our troubles started that day forward. Matt began to listen to the advice of some so-called nosy friends as well as some family members. They were telling him that the child was probably not his and that is why I had named him what I did. Unfortunately, I believe Matt began to believe the hype. Evidently, he started recapping our relationship, my sporadic distancing, my emotional disconnection and my roller coaster display of attitudes. He began to show his doubts that I had been unfaithful to him and that there was a possibility of the child belonging to someone else. But after all was said and done, I truly believed that Matt, his brother, and his mother knew in their heart that DaQuan was truly a Dilworth.

5

The Light Dims

Our rocky relationship was just that, rocky. We argued about stupid things, it did not matter, whatever it was became a real issue. So by the time DaQuan was about eight months old, I decided that I just could not do this relationship thing any more—I decided to bow out. Matt wanted to make it work and thought that we could work through it. But, not me, I was just too afraid and wanted to go my separate way.

I thought I wanted to be by myself, but my low self-esteem would not allow me. I ran into Vick and we started talking. I guess the conversation was sounding good as I made the mistake of rekindling the relationship for a third time. During this reconnection, I really believed that our relationship was good and that he would be committed to me. We ended up moving in together, all of which lasted about four months. While we were together, Matt would see Vick in my vehicle with other females and cheating as before. Matt told me of Vick's indiscretion; however, I would not believe him. I really believed that Matt had ulterior motives. I thought that he was just out to hurt me because I did not want to be with him. It seems my tract record of choosing a mate was still off because I was still choosing someone who wanted to hurt and disrespect me. This was becoming more evident when one day upon returning home; I noticed two glasses in the sink, one soiled with lipstick. I approached Vick about it but he insisted that it was a glass that I had left previously. I started putting things together and came to the conclusion that I had chosen wrong again. Things that family and other friends were saying were true, but you know that you really have to learn for yourself.

I got fed up, decided to leave the apartment. I moved out without him knowing. When he came home, all was gone and all the utilities were shut off. I returned to my parents' home. The place that I knew I would be welcomed, loved and treated well. Once again, I vowed to take care of DaQuan and myself. I knew that I had to realize who I was, and then begin to truly love myself. However, that lasted only a short period of time. I replayed the relationship tape of love as I let Stan back into the picture. He was home from school and just dropped in to say hello, to see how the family was doing. He said he was wondering how I was handling and enjoying being a mother. Lord, here I go again, back peddling into the same relational saddle again. We started dating, but deep down I had grown disheartened and frustrated with trying to make a relationship work by myself. I decided that enough was enough and gave Stan an ultimatum. I explained to him all that I had gone through in the past, including my relationship with him. I saw that Stan was fond of my son and I assumed that a close relationship could develop. I just could not let my son experience betrayal. I did not and would not allow my son to be exposed to someone popping in and out of his life emotionally. So, I gave him a year to make up his mind, either we were going to be a truly committed couple or we would go our separate ways. Of course, after a year's time, he was not ready to make that commitment, so I decided to move on!

6

New Beginnings

I was ready to learn *me*, to truly love *me*, to find out what Monique wanted out of life. I got tired of the same path I was constantly following and wanted to take a new journey in life. No longer did I want to feel the loneliness I was feeling. Now wanting to appreciate what life has to offer, I began to find myself by committing to be celibate. I was not going to give what was sacred to me to another man who did not appreciate the gift he had been given. I would remain celibate until God identified who my soul mate was, my husband. This was truly a challenge, but with God anything was possible. DaQuan now became my first priority instead of my relationships. No more would he be placed on the back burner. I realized that I was molding a life and by my examples I displayed, my son would surely follow my path or become someone he was not destined to be. I can remember during this time, DaQuan was about two years old, a man approached my Mom and I while we were in a Christian bookstore. DaQuan was dancing around and singing praises to God. The man noticed him and said to us, "That boy is destined to be somebody." That statement stuck with me and I was not going to ruin my son's life with my foolishness.

During this transitional period, Matt and I were seeing each other from time to time. The encounters were never sexual nor romantic as we were just being social and civilized in view of the fact that we were parents. However, being the Great Pretender, I was telling the family that I had no connections with Matt and referred to him as The Sperm Donor. Being deceitful was difficult and the stories got hard to keep up with. As time went along, I changed toward him and would not let Matt see DaQuan at all. My reason for doing this was because I started feeling that closeness again and believed my life was heading down the wrong path. I did not want to feel the imprisonment within myself. I felt if I stayed alone and kept my distance from him, I would not be in the same boat I had been in previously. I was afraid of being hurt. Instead of being totally honest, I just created more drama. During our break up, Matt had become involved and began seeing someone else, with whom he fathered a little girl, Miesha.

Doing some serious retrospection, I began to convince myself that it was okay to be alone. I began to pray to God and asked Him to remove some things from me, mostly, the self hate within, to help me learn to love me as I am and for what I am. I asked for God to put a man into my life that would love me for me! A man who would love me not for materialistic things nor would he want me only for the sex. I made a promise to God that I would no longer have sex with a guy until he was ready to give me his all in return. To give me what I wanted out of a committed and loving relationship. I prayed for strength to remain celibate until that special someone, my soul mate, who would be ready to give me what I truly deserved! My inner healing began.

A couple of months later, Matt's brother called and advised me that Matt had been arrested for drug possession. He stated that he was probably going to serve time, but was currently out on bail. I really did not think anything of it nor did I think it was anything major. My family was still under the impression that Matt and I were not on good terms. I constantly told them that I could not stand him and had nothing to do with him. But, my Dad was concerned that DaQuan was not seeing nor had a relationship with his father. One day, my Dad called me up to the bowling alley where he was bowling. When I got there, Matt was there. I froze, I really did not know what to say or do. It was an awkward situation, but little did I know that on this day I would see Matt as a free man for the last time. The next day, February 26, 1996, Matt went back to court and was found guilty. In March of 1996, he was sentenced to twenty five years in jail for drug possession with a minimum requirement of serving twelve and a half years.

During the first few months of his incarceration, I would talk to Matt when he called his brother. He was having a hard time coping with his situation and regretted where he ended up in life. I really had compassion for him and felt sorry that we had not worked things out as a couple. I regretted how I had denied him a relationship with his son regardless of what we were going through. I regretted and felt bad that DaQuan had not had a chance to develop a relationship with his father. I had listened too much to what some family members had advised me to do instead of following my heart and doing what was right for my son. From time to time, I would go to visit Matt and take DaQuan with me. Obviously, with Matt being incarcerated, the relationship was platonic, but all things worked together for good. We actually learned how to be adults, becoming civilized as two individuals should do when they have a common thread, our son. We learned the art of communication as we became true friends over the next year. We learned to listen to each other and share what we both wanted out of the life: the life that was left before us as individuals and as parents to our son. Some might think it was a little too late, but not us. We believed that it is really never too late to contribute to the gift of life that was given to us. We did what we had to do, thank God we were maturing.

While maturing emotionally, I began to mature spiritually. My conversations and relationship grew with God. I truly believe that God had given me a word that Matt was the one for me, but with this belief came frustration and to be honest, anger. Here it is I have prayed and asked God for a man to love me for me, but that man is locked up!! Even though I did not specifically ask for the man to be by my side, there is no way that you could have told me that Matt would be the one who was chosen to give me that unconditional love now. Look what we have been through, look where we came from and look where he is currently! How could this truly be the man for me? No way! However, God kept placing it in my heart that, yes, he is the one and the one with whom you would share your life. I guess it is true that you must learn to be more specific when praying. Yes, I prayed and asked God for the man but some of these details were not obvious to me at the time. As time grew, so did our relationship. It grew as a nurturing seed that is watered, groomed and nourished, it blossomed! It was not this way in our previous relationship, as we just jumped into it too fast. We did not allow a true friendship to build, prior to becoming intimate. But strange as it seemed, this time everything felt right.

After a couple of years, Matt asked me to marry him, I said "Yes". However, he felt that he needed to write my parents a letter. He wrote a letter to them apologizing for all the stupid things we did as a couple and the foolishness we put our son through. Matt wanted them to know that he was truly committed to our relationship and that they had no need of worrying about me getting hurt. This truly meant a lot to me, even though majority of the problems were my fault.

Needless to say, a lot of people talked about me and disapproved of my decision. They were saying, "You must be crazy! I can't believe you are actually going to mess up your life. Matt is locked up, why stop your life to wait for him until he serves his time?" At first, I did start to listen and began to show doubt, questioning my decision. But after a while, I had to realize that this was exactly my problem in past years, letting others dictate how and what I should do. Always allowing others to manipulate me and allowing them to change my directions. I really never did what I truly wanted to do. I never made choices in my life that I felt provided me with the happiness that I wanted. I was always too busy trying to please friends and family, allowing them to make decisions for me. But not this time, I vowed to stand tall to whatever my decision was and what I thought was good enough for me. No matter what anyone felt, no matter what they believed, no matter what was said or how I would be judged, I would not care. No longer would I allow anyone to dictate my life choices, nor change my mind, no matter if they agreed with me or not. As far as I was concerned, they had no say—they had to butt out, after all, was it not my life anyway?!?

Our relationship was like any other platonic one, Matt and I had agreements and disagreements; we had ups and we had downs. But overall, we were connecting even though the green eyed monster (jealousy) at times appeared in some episodes. Even though Matt and the mother of his second daughter had gone their separate ways,

I was still uncomfortable. I was the one with the issues of him having other children and two other Baby Mamas. But these were some things I knew I had to deal with if I was going to be with Matt. If I was willing to take him as being the "One", then I knew that I had to take the whole package of him, his children and yes, even the two mothers. I could not pick and choose. If the kids were in his life, then they were in mine too. Was it easy, not at all, I would be lying if I said yes. It was difficult at first, with him having a relationship with both of his daughters, but after some adjustments, compromising and submissions, we began to get along. As time passed, I learned to love them both and consider both of them as my daughters as well. I also have a relationship with their mothers and other family members. God is truly good.

7

The Storm Begins

The year 1999 was a very difficult year. In January, Matt found out that his only brother Myron had also been incarcerated for a crime he said he did not commit and was also facing twenty five years with a minimal serving time of twelve and a half years. Adding to Matt's sorrow and depression, about eight months later, Matt found out that his mother had to have surgery to have some tumors removed. However, he did not know that she in fact had colon cancer. She did not want to worry him with her illness and she knew if I knew, I would inform Matt. Along with his depression was his agony of not being by his mother's side during her need. Matt felt helpless because he was unable to give her a hug and a kiss and to be able to tell her it was going to be okay. This reminded him of how helpless his Mom felt when his Dad was sick and died ten years earlier.

On October 20, 1999, I had received a call at work from one of Matt's cousins. He told me that Mama Ora had died. I left work rushing to his Mom's house. On the way there, all I could think about was Matt, Myron and the grandchildren. Mama Ora normally worked during the day and would not be home. Therefore, when I got there, it was strange that Matt called. I answered the phone not knowing it was him and just froze. After accepting the call, he stated "Monique, where is Mama." I couldn't say anything. He said, "Monique, Mama is dead isn't she?" I told him yes. He began to break down and became angry. I knew he needed me. I got off of the phone and got in my car and took that hour and a half drive to be with my man. When I got there, I explained to the guards what had happened. They gave us a private room. I can remember Matt coming in with tears in his eyes and just hugging me and not letting go. He said that we were all he had now, besides his brother. I stayed for about one hour and knew I had to go and tell DaQuan. He was very close to her. When I got home I told him that his Grandma Ora had died. He cried intensely because this was the first death he had experienced. A week prior to her death, DaQuan had given her a pink pig. He told her that the pig would help her tumors. She gave DaQuan a radio headphone set that same day. She told him that this was probably the last gift she would give him. She knew then she was dying, but we were completely in the dark. When she died the pig was in the bed with her. To this day, DaQuan has the pink pig and the radio headphone set.

At first, Matt felt that with both parents gone and with his only brother locked up too, he was all alone. But as time passed, he knew he could count on me. We became one in mind, heart and spirit. This time a true connection had developed, not just in a sexual way as before.

August of 2000, my Dad, Mom, DaQuan and I went on a family trip to Florida. During this trip, I was experiencing symptoms of fatigue and thirst. While driving I would fall asleep at the wheel and would have to pull over to let someone else drive. I knew one thing for certain, my tiredness was not due to any pregnancy, I was celibate. I thought perhaps, the thirst was from the weather change. I just did not know what was going on with me, just could not figure it out. I really did not want to go to the doctor nor did I want to find out any negative news. However, my Mom persisted and I ended up making an appointment upon my return home. In October of 2000, I was diagnosed with Type II Diabetes. My blood sugar was tested at 460, which was extremely high and out of control. I really did not know the importance of the blood sugar level and all, but I knew that I was very depressed at the news! I was distraught and angry because at the young age of twenty-seven, I had diabetes!! This is something that my Grandmother had, plus other older people I knew!! Dealing with this diagnosis was really hard for me and I must admit that I was in denial. I knew that this was something that I had to deal with for the rest of my life and some life changes had to be made. Little did I know that this was just the beginning of some life-altering changes.

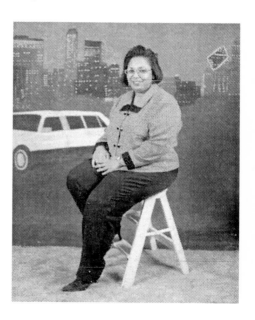

Approximately, three years or so later, I began to have some heavy bleeding and terrible menstrual cramps. I would bleed so heavy that it required me to wear two overnight sanitary napkins. It was just unbearable. I went to my OB/GYN to find out what was going on. In 2003, I was told that I had about four or five fibroid tumors. They said that it was not really mandatory to have them removed but if I wanted some relief from the heavy bleeding and cramps, it was recommended. I was also told that being a diabetic, risks were involved with surgery. The risks involved were improper or slow healing and possible infections. In addition, there was a twenty 25 percent chance of the tumors returning. But to me, it would be worth it for the relief. I would just pray that the 75 percent would override the possibility of their return and that there would be no complications.

In April of 2003, I had to my surprise seventeen tumors removed. Two were the size of a grapefruit and fifteen others clustered around them. This turned out to be a major surgery. Because I had lost so much blood during surgery, a blood transfusion of two pints was required. I stayed in the hospital about four days then they sent me home. However, around Easter I became very ill. I could not keep anything on my stomach and had reoccurring diarrhea. I was so weak I could not even hold my head up. When my Mom rushed me to the emergency room, I had a high fever, my blood pressure was low and I was dehydrated. I remained in the hospital another seven days. They were unable to pin point the problem. All they knew was that I did in fact have an infection. Being confined in the hospital made me frustrated and angry because I wanted to be home! Although the risks of surgery were known ahead of time, I really did not think that it would happen to me. Needless to say, I was not a good patient. I was snappy, whiny and irritable to the medical staff and my family.

They conducted a vaginal biopsy without anesthesia of which proved to be the most excruciating pain that I had ever experienced. I could not understand why I was going through this and why this was happening to me. To top that, the doctors came in one day and stated that it might be better for me to go ahead and have a hysterectomy. I was by myself at the time and I was scared. I cried and cried as I really did not want to have this finalization of childbirth. I was still considering having another child once Matt and I were married. I thought this procedure would be the worse thing ever and I was totally against it. Therefore, they decided to send me home with a Pick-line IV to continue treatment for the infection. This procedure called for a line to be connected to my vein in order for antibiotic medicines to be administered. I had to have treatments around the clock. My Mom was still working, so my Dad, who was retired, took the responsibility of administering my medicine throughout the day and evening. I was off work for eight weeks. After returning for a follow-up with my doctor, the infection was gone and everything was great. However, I was still having heavy periods and pain. I decided to try and deal with it as long as I could.

8

In The Midst

The year of 2004 had proven to be very stressful and busy. On June 29th, I was working from home; my office was in the basement. My Mom was at a meeting at church. DaQuan was in the kitchen watching television and my grandmother, Mildred Carter Burnette (known to DaQuan as G.G.) was sitting in her bedroom. My Dad's whereabouts were unknown. While working, I heard a big thump and was wondering what in the world was DaQuan doing. But DaQuan calls me as he was running down the stairs, saying, "Mom, Mom, G.G. fell, G.G. fell on the floor." I came running up the stairs. As I got to the bedroom, I saw my grandmother lying on the floor. She had something running out of her mouth and when I touched her, she was ice cold. I was so scared; I did not know what to do. I was hysterical and in a frenzy. I called an aunt and then called 9ll to tell them that my grandmother had fallen and that she was not responding. I opened the front door and begin screaming, "Help, Help!" This is when I realized my Dad was on the porch. He told me to go get my Mom from church. When I arrived at church the first person I saw was Auntie April (my Mom's best friend). I told her what had happened. She went to the room where my Mom was in and physically pulled her out of the room. I was so shaken that I could not drive. Auntie April drove my car and my Mom drove hers. When we got back to the house, the paramedics had my grandmother on a stretcher to take her to the nearest hospital. I always told my Mom that if anything ever happened to G.G., I prayed that I would not be the one to find her. I did not but my son did.

All of the adults went to the hospital while DaQuan went over a cousin's house to stay until we returned. All the way to the hospital, my mind ran across the events of that day. I was nervous and did not know what to expect or think. My grandmother and I did not always see eye-to-eye. There were some jealous issues that we had to work through. We both strived for my Mom's attention and it seemed we were always in competition. We were known for going back and forth on anything and everything. I tried to recollect if we had had an argument that day or not. I was wondering what was our last conversation or last words we said to each other. Were we mean or said hurtful things to each other that day? It was all such a blur now.

It seemed the wait in the emergency room was an eternity. All of the family, some close friends, and my Pastor arrived to be with us in the Family Waiting Room. The news had spread fast. The wait was agonizing. It was an hour or so before the Chaplain from the hospital came into the room. I knew at that moment that something was not right. Behind the Chaplain was the doctor who stated that my grandmother was gone. I fell to my knees as I just felt that I was emptied and a big void had just happened. It was the hardest thing to deal with. The last death that I had to experience was my Dad's father in 1990. He was sick and hospitalized before he died. I was the youngest granddaughter to graduate from high school. It hurt because his death prevented him from seeing me go on prom and graduate. But, now to have someone you love taken instantly like that from you was a hard pill to swallow.

We had G.G's funeral on July 6, 2004. DaQuan, being such a strong-willed and spirited boy that he was, had spoken at her funeral. He did such an awesome job. I was so proud of him. He has always been outspoken, articulate and has always shown his love for God.

Times were very difficult, but we had to endure and keep going on. I was trying to get through this ordeal for myself. I was going over all the silly things we argued about and wishing to say, "I'm sorry." But, it's too late now. I knew that I needed to be a support for my Mom. I knew she was hurting inside but she did not seem to express it outwardly.

In January of 2005, I went for my regular examinations to see the OB/GYN doctor that performed my surgery. I advised her that I was still having very heavy bleeding, terrible cramps and that it was getting unbearable to deal with every month. I asked her for some options to a reasonable resolution, of which she suggested the birth control patch, the OrthoEvra. I followed her recommendation and the periods did lighten up and my cramps were not as bad. Ok, finally some relief. During this time too, she had given me a general exam of my breast. As she was examining me, she felt a small lump. But she said not to worry. It was probably due to my upcoming menstrual cycle which was due in a week or so. I was told that this was normal to feel changes in your breast upon the approaching of your cycle. So, with her being the trained professional, I trusted her knowledge. I had just turned thirty-two years old at the time, so I did not think anymore about it nor did I feel concerned.

About February of 2005, I was watching a special on the television program, Dateline. They were covering the story of a girl who was on the same birth control patch that I was on. This drew my attention as it stated that she had developed complications, had a stroke and died from this patch. Immediately, I got scared and took the patch off. I did not want to wonder what complications I could possibly endure from it. I had already taken birth control for many years from the ages of fifteen to nineteen. I had gone from the birth control pill to the Depo-Provera shot which made me sick and gave me symptoms related to pregnancy. So I figured enough was enough. I decided against taking any further birth control medicines, especially in view of the fact that I was not sexually active anyway. I had to stop and take consideration to what I was doing to my body. In many conversations, Matt and I had talked extensively about how we were both getting older. We discussed our potential financial hardships and situation. The both of us decided that additional children would probably not be an option. Therefore, I consulted my doctor to seek an option of sterilization.

So in May of 2005, my OB/GYN doctor referred me over to another specialist regarding the sterilization option. After examination, the specialist indicated that he could not do a vaginal nor abdominal cut due to so many scar tissues that were present from my previous surgery. He did advise of another procedure where they could go through the tubes through the vagina to perform sterilization. The procedure had to be performed within a certain time period after my menstrual. However, there was no guarantee that it would work on the first time and it might require a second attempt. My insurance company would only cover the first attempt, but not the second, so this would cause a financial strain as the surgery was costly. Additionally, this procedure was proved to be problematic because my menstrual cycles were not regulated. Therefore, I could not schedule an appointment in a timely manner. So, this option was not an option for me. Here I go again, confronting another wall of frustration.

My Uncle, Michael Morrison, had been very sick; as a matter of fact, even though he was weak, he had attended my grandmother's funeral. Uncle Michael was diagnosed with colon cancer. He was really dealing with it and trying to hold on and be strong for Aunt Martha and my cousins. On top of this, my other grandmother (Dad's Mom) had become very ill and had taken a turn for the worse. She had become bed-ridden and unable to eat. She was very weak and began to suffer from hallucinations. The family had started to take turns to attend and care for her at home. As strange as it seems, this probably pleased Grandmamma to have her family at her home almost everyday. Even in her state of mind, it seemed she would often take a motherly roll-call of her kids. She would periodically call out one of the kid's name of which they would respond.

9

HURRICANE "CATERGORY 5"

The second week of July, my immediate family and I had gone to Denver for a family member's wedding. While getting dressed for the wedding, I noticed a difference in my left breast. My left breast was larger than my right one. I did a self-examination and felt a small lump. I remembered what my doctor had told me before. It was about that time, so I figured it must be due to an upcoming cycle, so do not worry.

A few weeks later, on July 25th, my Uncle Michael lost his fight with colon cancer. He was a close uncle whom I loved and knew he loved me. Again, another hard situation to deal with, another void and another lost. So many things were happening, so many disappointments, and so many losses. Why was life taking such a spiral turn right now? Why were so many people being taken away from us? What the heck was going on? What was happening to us as a family?

As time went on, when I would lay down at night to go to sleep, it was difficult to lie on my left breast. It would hurt something awful. In August, I decided to go to my primary care physician to get it checked out. When she checked my breast, the lump was larger. Not only was the lump larger, but my skin started to feel and look like an orange peel. It really felt rough on my left side. She questioned if I had a history of breast cancer in my immediate family. I told her all I knew about at the time was my great-grandmother on my Dad's side and my great-aunt on my Mom's side who had breast cancer. To my knowledge, there was no closer history. She decided to have me go for a mammogram and ultrasound anyway, just to be sure. Insurance companies do not approve of such procedures for women under the age of forty without history of cancer in the immediate family.

On August 11 2005, I went to the hospital to have the mammogram. Upon reading of the x-ray, the radiologist stated that there seem to be something suspicious but without further review could not positively say one way or another. So, they performed an ultrasound which identified something abnormal. They wanted me to schedule a biopsy to confirm their suspicions. But I told them of an upcoming planned vacation just two days away. (I was taking DaQuan, Miesha and Veronica to Florida for a week.) Therefore, they decided to do the biopsy that day. I was extremely nervous and I called my Mom to come to the hospital to be with me. That biopsy was excruciating! They cut both my breast, without anesthesia, to take tissue out for their examination. To add to that agony, I would have to wait for the results of these tests.

So I went on vacation with the kids. I tried not to think about anything or about the upcoming results of my tests. I just wanted to keep my mind focused and to keep a positive attitude hoping that nothing is going to be wrong. Things would be okay, everything is going to be fine.

I returned on August 20th, however, I had not heard anything from the doctor nor the hospital. My Mom and Dad were leaving out for Puerto Vallarta, Mexico as I was returning from vacation. On Monday, August 22nd, I got a call from my doctor who told me that I did in fact have breast cancer. I was so confused, upset, and was just numb, not knowing what to do. My Mom and Dad were not at home, they were many miles away in a far off distant land. I was all alone at home. I felt like my world had ended. Again, I questioned why I had to go through so much in my life at such a young age. I did not understand what was happening to me nor why. I immediately got on the telephone and called my parents in Mexico. I could hear the worry and fear in my parent's voice. I knew that they were just as frightened as I was. Initially I was told it could have been in the early stage of cancer and it was good that I found it when I did. My girl cousins came to be with me and to take me to the doctor to obtain a referral to see exactly what was going on and where I stood physically. Nothing would be known for certain until a meeting with the surgeon.

I had previously told Matt of the test I had to take and was waiting for the results. I can remember him calling the day I found out. To demonstrate our oneness and spirit, Matt seemed to always call when something devastating had occurred. When I told him, he had gotten silent. I could hear the nervousness and worry in his voice. I am quite sure all he could think about was his Mom dying from colon cancer. He assured me that everything was going to be fine and he was in my corner 100 percent.

The separation from my parents seemed to be the longest ever. When they came home, all we could do was hug and cry. The next week, I met with the surgeon. My Mom accompanied me. He was very outspoken and told me exactly what the situation was and what I needed to hear. He did not sugar coat anything, but was direct and honest. From his conversation, I knew he trusted and believed in a higher power, he believed in God. But when he looked at the papers and the x-rays, he told me that I was at Stage Three of cancer. At first, I did not understand what that meant. I know now that there are four stages of cancer and mine was really aggressive. He told me that I had two options and that I had to have a strong and focused mind if I wanted to live. Here I am thirty-two years old, sitting in a doctor's office scared and he's telling me that I had two options. Then he told me of my options—one option was removing the lump with the possibility of the lump and cancer returning, or the other option was having a complete mastectomy, the total removal of the left breast. Thereafter, I could have reconstructive surgery to reform the breast. I thought back to when I had the fibroid tumors removed, with the 25 percent chance of them returning. Since I knew that I was dealing with cancer, I knew that I did not want to deal with the possibility of its return. My experience of cancer, my uncle dying and Matt's Mom dying of cancer, I just did not want to chance it. Even though I was scared out of my mind, I decided to have my breast removed. Why, oh why I kept asking myself. Why me? What have I done to deserve such a life? Why did I have to feel so much suffering and pain? I did not understand.

10

Why, Why, Why?

My surgery was scheduled on October 14, 2005. Needless to say, the waiting period was frightening. All I could think about was my son. Am I going to be here to live? Will I be here for him? Will I be able to see him grow up? Will I see him go to high school? Or to prom? Or will I even be there when he gets married? If I had many questions, I am sure that DaQuan had some too. I was just so worried and concerned for him and his well-being. I knew I had to have open communication with him. I sat DaQuan down and talked to him honestly and openly. I explained to him what was going on with me. I advised him all that was going to be done. I really thought that he would break down and cry. However, my strong son took his Holy Bible, read a scripture about having faith and told *me* how God was going to be there to protect me. Here I am the adult, thirty-two years old and I am the one scared. I do not know what is going on, but my son who was eleven and a half is speaking to *me* about faith and how *I* needed to express that faith—so a child shall lead.

It is now the end of August, all during this time, as I stated, my Dad's Mom had been sick and now was not responding as much. On August 30, 2005, the family gathered at her house to celebrate her eighty sixth birthday. However, I really do not think she was conscious of it as she seemed to be drifting away. She was going through a lot. She seemed to be suffering and refused to eat any-

39

thing. She went from July to September without any food, just very few liquids, a sip here or there.

One of the family members, much to my dissatisfaction had told Grandmamma what I was going through. Upon my next visit, even though now she was not talking a lot, I could see in her face the grave concern that she had for me. I could see the worry in her eyes that she had for me as she held my hand. But she knew and believed that Someone else had me in His arms. In one of her talkative moments, I remember sitting in the room alone with her; we were just making small talk. In an effort to make her laugh, I would say, "Grandmamma, nobody is in here but me and you, you can tell me now that I am your favorite." She would say, "No, baby, I don't have any favorites. I love you all the same." She further stated her whole concern was about the family staying together, loving each other and remaining close. She had her way. Throughout her sickness, the family gathered almost every day to see about her and to play games to pass the time. On September 13, 2005, Grandmamma, Dallas Mayetta Rhea was taken from me. But this time, I did not feel as sad as when my first grandmother had died. I saw this grandmother suffer for so long, from July to September. All she ever wanted to know was that her family would stay together and that Uncle LeVoyd would be okay. We had her funeral on September 21, 2005. At the grave site, we felt the release and peace as we were standing there. The sun was shining and all of a sudden a brisk wind came with a slight mist of rain. We knew she was swept away to her heavenly home, even through the mist of our tears.

On October 13, 2005, the night before my surgery, I could not sleep. I knew my time was near for me to have my surgery, in becoming a little less of a normal woman. I was so stressed and so worried. I knew in my heart that I was in God's hands, but I was truly scared. The surgery day had arrived. My Mom, Rev. Francine Stark and my Aunt Francine was there comforting me. But in my mind, I was not ready to go in for this surgery because I had not yet seen my Dad and Renell (brother). Soon as they were about to roll me into the Operating Room, both of them walked in, just in time. Now, my spirit was ready and I was a little more at ease. I came out of surgery okay; they removed my breast, twenty four lymph nodes (all cancerous) and placed a tissue expander in at the same time. I felt the love on the day of surgery because I had twenty two family members, friends and ministerial staff from my church present in the hospital waiting room, almost a family member per lymph node. They all represented the cause and uphill battle against cancer by wearing pink. This was so awesome to have people who cared and demonstrated their love for me during this rough time. My roommate in the hospital asked me if all of these people were here for me. She also wanted to know if I just found out that I had cancer. I told her no, they had known for a while but just wanted to be here in support. That's what our family does.

I came home the next day after surgery which demonstrated to everyone how strong I was. I had to be strong for my son and family, but mainly for my son. However, it took me about four or five days before I could remove the dressing to take a look at myself. The first time that I did look and saw only one breast, I was devastated. I felt ugly and disfigured. I felt abnormal and that nobody would love me as I was, especially Matt, now that I only had one breast. But Matt remained supportive during this time and expressed his support through calls and letters. He told me many times that it did not matter about me having one breast, he loved me for me. This was comforting; however, I still felt less—less than whole.

I had to meet with the oncologist to see what was to be the mode of treatment now that surgery was over. Because the cancer was so aggressive and me being so young, they took a lot of precautions with me. At first, I was under the impression that I would take chemotherapy for two to three months. I figured that I could do that and it would be okay. I had a PET Scan performed in November 2005 to check for any additional signs of cancer. They identified that cancer had developed in the left lung. However, they decided to wait until I had completed all of the cycles of chemo to see if this would cure it. So on November 11, 2005, I began my treatments. I had a mediport placed in my chest for the issuance of the chemotherapy. This was recommended to ensure that I was able to take the chemo properly and having the port was better than going through the vein each time. I really did not know what to expect, but I was warned that my hair would definitely fall out. The dose and strength of the medicine was a tough one. My hair was long at the time, so to eliminate such a dramatic change, I had it cut short.

11

Killing, Restoring & Infuriating

The first treatment was very difficult. I was very, very weak and so tired after treatment. The treatment kills all cells, cancerous as well as good ones. This took a big toll on my body; I vomited all night. After, three days of this, I had to be readmitted to the hospital because I had become dehydrated. I was released after four days and was resting at home. One day while brushing my hair, big clumps of hair began to come out in the brush. Every time I would even touch my head or run my fingers through it, hair would be in my hand. It became very thin on top. So, I decided to go to the beauty shop and have it cut as close as possible. Coming home, looking in the mirror, now seeing an almost bald head and one breast, the look tore me up badly inside. But I knew that I had to continue to stay strong and to keep pressing on. I had to keep doing what I had to do. I refuse to let the devil know or think that he was going to get the better of me. I knew that God had me, but I was still so angry!! I was frustrated with God; I did not understand why He was allowing this to happen!

I remember a conversation with my Mom in the kitchen with just the two of us being at home one day. I expressed my anger and disappointment with God. Why did I have to have cancer? Why did all of my loved ones have to be taken away from me? Why did I have to deal with all the things that I was going through? I did not understand, I was mad and wanted everyone to know it. I just wanted a sense of relief, wanted everything negative, bad and evil just taken away. I remembered being frustrated, became quiet and non-communicative. I stayed to myself, not really wanting to be bothered with anyone, nor wanting to hear what anyone had to say.

The two months of chemo turned into six months. The first cycle of chemo was a three month period. I would do that once every three weeks and until I finished the 4th cycle of the chemo, always going the following day for a shot to boost my white blood cells. Then the second dose of chemo, I took this every week for sixteen weeks with a one week break in between. This medicine did not make me as sick as the first cycle; however, it made my body ache like crazy. My joints would hurt so bad, it would hurt to walk. Time seemed hard for me. Every month, lab work was performed to check my markers; this would tell me if the cancer levels were high or low. All during this time, from November 2005 to June 2006, one marker would always remain a little high. I never really had normal markers.

January 2006, my family gave me a surprise birthday party. I really needed that! I needed some sense of happiness and pleasure. But what my family really did not see on the outside was what I was going through on the inside was a state of depression. I was going through a lot, thinking a lot, always in deep thought. I was still angry and frustrated with life and the way mine was going. I felt like it was just too hard. So May 2006, I decided to seek counseling and see a psychiatrist. I needed to talk about my feelings and my problems. I was in an out-patient treatment program which lasted for two weeks. I went to group therapy every day, Monday through Friday. During therapy, I began to tell my story and to hear others' stories. While sharing my story of how I was trying to stay strong in all that I had gone through, I started to feel a difference. I said, "Okay, something is changing here". As I was telling my story, I remembered a question the doctor asked me that constantly rang in my ear ever since then. He asked, "Monique, do you know what your purpose in life is?" I could not answer the question!! I really did not know what my purpose in life was and I did not know what he meant by that question. What was he trying to get me to see or know? I did not know then but now I know that he was trying to get me to dig deeper into my soul for the answer. What is your purpose Monique? What does God have for you and what does He want you to do?

During the course of the therapy, I began feeling so much better, a new sense of self started to develop. When I would think of myself as disfigured or deformed on the outside, I would dig deeper to identify that I was totally whole on the inside. Yes, I may have had cancer, but I am still alive. Yes, I have had suffering, but along with the suffering, there is healing. So I began to understand that things happen for a reason and because things happen for a reason, you have to learn to deal with it and move on.

After group therapy, DaQuan and I began individual therapy. My depression began to have a negative impact on him as well. His grades in school began to decline and he began to misbehave. DaQuan was also very concerned with my health. It was not until his counseling, that I found out that he would get up in the middle of the night to check to see if I was still alive. It was heartbreaking to know that he was suffering just as much as I was. This was too much for him to bear and go through. But being the child of God he is, he remained strong for his Mom.

The female therapist that I had was very good. As a matter of fact, every physician that I had consulted throughout my treatments, all knew God, knew Who He was and was not ashamed to confess their belief in Him. They admitted that it was He that would do the healing, not them. During one session with the therapist, my Mom had the opportunity to join us and express her feelings. Anyone who knows my Dad knows this was not his cup of tea. I respected his feelings. I was happy about this because she never expressed her feelings to me before. She stated that she was hurting and scared and did not want to see me suffer. Seeing her emotions let me know that she indeed could express her pain. I knew my Dad was scared and wondered why his baby had to go through so much. I knew that they too were going through a lot as well as I.

It was a time in therapy that I expressed to my therapist that as time approached for me to get another PET Scan, I would get nervous and antsy; always did when it was time to obtain the results of the test. My therapist made a profound statement to me, "When you get the results of your scan, LET GO AND LET GOD. WHAT CAN YOU CHANGE?" Right then, I realized that if it did come back as something that I did not want to hear, there *is* nothing I can do to change it. I have to take what comes and go with it. I have to endure in order to make it. I had to keep pushing on. I cannot change anything; I must trust and believe. Also during this cancer season, I stopped going to church. My reason for stopping was due to the reactions of people. They made me feel that I was on my death bed. I know it was something that I was internalizing personally, but when they would come to me they would say things as, "Oh, baby, I am sooo sorry. All you have to do is just trust God." But during my angry stages, I wanted to tell them that they do not know what I am going through! How can you tell me what I should do? You can not tell me how I am supposed to feel! Do not tell me what I am supposed to do! You are not walking in my shoes! You do not understand my struggles! Even those women who had had cancer five to twenty years ago would try to comfort me, but I had no connection. I could not connect because they were all in their late forties and fifties. I felt that they did not have the same issues that I had as a younger woman. I could not understand them or hear them. I felt I was so much younger and was the only one in my age group going through this. There was no one around in my age group who knew or understood what I felt! I AM ANGRY!! I thought and felt that I was singled out and all alone.

12

Bring It On

When it came to my appointments and treatment, both my Mom and Dad would take alternate turns in taking me to chemo. They were there for me every step of the way. They are some of the best parents anyone could ever ask for. I really do not know what I would have done throughout this whole ordeal without such caring parents. They have been there in times when I really needed them to be and sometimes when I did not. I have grown to love and cherish them so much because they have been there no matter what the sacrifice or cost to them. Every single appointment, every treatment, either one or both was in attendance; I was never alone—they were there. I thank God for the blessing of such wonderful parents.

My son, DaQuan, has been super and inspirational, even at his young age. He has been very attentive and concerning to my needs and wants. My family as a whole, friends and church family were supportive and encouraging as well.

In June of 2006, I saw my oncologist and of course my Mom accompanied me. He sat me down with the results of the PET Scan. He advised me that I would have to go through another *four months of chemotherapy*!! The test confirmed what they saw previously in November 2005. The cancer came back in my left upper lung!! My first reaction was to cry. Oh my God! Not again! Not more of this same agony! But even though, it was devastating news, I was not as frustrated as I had thought I would be. I cried, but knew I would now have to stand firmer on God's word. I knew that I had to believe and trust that the Lord would heal me. I would not let the devil have any victory over my life—*NO VICTORY IN THIS BAT-*

TLE!! I would leave this battle for the Lord to handle. It is His, not mine!! So this time when the doctor stated another four months, I replied, "Okay, Lord, sign me up, let's do this! I am ready to take on the next challenges that you have for me and I know that I will be okay!" I must say that my oncologist is such a wonderful guy who is straightforward, honest and a believer. Although, a learned man of medicine, he always gives God the victory over everything.

I was scheduled to start my next dose of chemo in the early part of June but we were planning a Family Reunion of which was to take place that month. As I was the coordinator, I asked if it were possible to attend the reunion and then return to start my treatments. My oncologist said okay. By this time, my hair had begun to return and it was returning in a totally different grade and texture. A lot of family members were teasing me saying it was more like my Mom's this time, not like my Dad's—this became a family joke.

Well, I attended the reunion with Families United and had a great time. You see, back in the late 1970's my family vowed to stay united and remain close. They organized a group called *Families United*. This group consists of brothers, sisters, in laws, cousins, nieces, nephews, extended family and the list goes on. They felt this was one way of keeping our bond and continuing on with the generations to come. *Families United* gives parties, picnics, reunions, cruises and whatever it takes to keep us as one.

The reunion was truly awesome! To be with family members whom you never met and those you have known all of your life was a blessing. It was more awesome for me in view of my current situation, medically as well as emotionally. I needed that connection, that feeling of belonging and being loved. The reunion was a weekend affair. That Saturday night was a dinner dance. Much to my surprise, I was being honored. My family had gotten together and had given me a beautiful crystal clock, saying "Job Well Done" from *Families United*. Also, about thirteen little cousins and my niece presented me with a rose and a hug. The last person to honor me was my son, DaQuan. He grabbed me and held me so tight, as if he never wanted to let me go. This was truly heart-warming as I love my son so much and I know my son loves me. I just broke down and cried. There we were embracing and crying together. All of my female family members surrounded DaQuan and me. They called my Dad and Mom to join us. All of the family stood in one accord, pleading and praying to God for my healing. Praying for my deliverance, praying for me to be well, to claim and walk into whatever God had for me in life. That was such an inspiring experience for me. I felt the presence of God. I felt His love and compassion in that room. I felt the love of my family. They expressed that love by their words of comfort, encouragement, and support. It was truly wonderful. Words can never express how I felt that day and what it all meant to me.

Upon returning from the reunion, I prepared to go for my next round of chemotherapy. This dose did in fact make me nauseated, but not sick to point of vomiting or hospitalization. However, as before it affected my ability to walk. Previously, it took about a week or so before my hair began to fall out. This time, it only took 2 days before the shedding started. So, I made a choice to beat it before it beat me. I went to the bathroom along with my daughter, Miesha and we shaved the rest of my hair off that day. I refused to get frustrated or mad with something that I had no control over. I decided to take control instead. No weapons formed against me would prosper and surely the devil would not have the victory! I declared that I *was* going to be well and that I *was* moving onward in this battle. There was nothing and no one who could hold me back!

13

Not Alone

I finished the last four months of chemo with a positive mind, spirit and body. As I was going through this treatment, I began to talk with other patients who were in the room with me. Previously, I would remain quiet and kept to myself. Now I found myself listening to their stories and really hearing them. I met a guy who was twenty-two years old and diagnosed with testicular cancer, a woman who was thirty-four years old with breast cancer and another woman, thirty-seven years old was diagnosed with breast cancer that had spread to her lungs and bones. She was Stage Four. I began to realize that I *was* not alone that there were other people out there just like me with cancer at a young age. Earlier, I felt as if I was the only one in the world because, at first, all I came in contact with were older people. Along with this chemo, I had radiation for five and a half weeks, every day, Monday through Friday. However, this was extended to eight weeks because my skin burned so badly. I had to take a rest in between the radiation treatments.

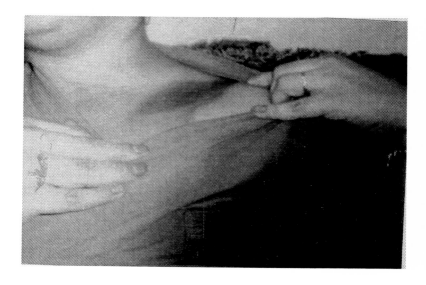

During the cycles of chemo and radiation, I also had to have tissue expansions done. This was injected saline which gradually stretched the breast tissue to try to match the size of the right breast. So, I am here to tell you that it *was* a struggle, it *was hard* and completely painful. But I was willing to move forward because I knew that God was in control of it all. I had to stand firm in knowing who I was and Whose I was. I knew that in order to be healed, I had to have high spirits, believe, and trust in God.

October of 2006 made a year of undergoing everything—surgeries, chemotherapy treatments, and radiation. I had another PET Scan performed and an appointment was scheduled to obtain the results of the scan as well as my markers for cancer. My parents were away on their annual vacation trip, so my cousin accompanied me on this visit. I was not worried or afraid even though I had some people to ask ignorant questions as, "What if the cancer returns? What would you do?" The only logical response was, "WHAT

COULD I DO?" Is there really anything that I could do or change? All I could do is believe that whatever God has for me to go through that I had to rest in the knowing that He is in the midst of it all.

So my cousin and I are at the oncologist's office. I must admit that even though feeling confident, the waiting to receive the report was a little rough. But, PRAISE GOD, the scan revealed no cancer was evident in my body and my markers were normal, Hallelujah!! However, it was not until this visit that I learned that the cancer had advanced to Stage Four when it had spread to the lung area.

My oncologist spoke with me about some preventative measures. He explained that because I was so young with still so much estrogen in my body, further precautions needed to be considered. Therefore, he suggested that I should have a partial hysterectomy, removing of the ovaries only. This would reduce the risk of ovarian cancer. I agreed and met with the OB/GYN the same day. He advised me of all the details of the surgery. Upon the examination by this doctor, I found out that my fibroid tumors had returned. Therefore, a full hysterectomy, the removal of all female organs, was recommended. This was a concern from both doctors due to my age and only having one child. But, I chose life with the blessing of one child rather than further complications with my health. With upcoming breast reconstruction and breast reduction, I decided to have the hysterectomy all done on the same day. The right breast reduction was decided because I could no longer tolerate any additional painful tissue expansions in the left breast. An additional vaginal biopsy was required prior to this surgery to assure that no presence of ovarian cancer. All was fine and we were ready for surgery.

During this period I had an encounter with the Holy Spirit. I was lying in my bed. I was in the house all alone; suddenly I felt God's presence around me. I knew it was Him because the presence was peaceful and reassuring. It was strange because I had never felt this before. I had questioned for so long what my purpose was that God was finally going to tell me. He whispered in my ear, *Why God Chose Me*. I immediately jumped up thinking someone was in the house. But I realized that the alarm was on and I was all alone. I laid back down and closed my eyes. Again He whispered, *Why God Chose Me*. I finally realized what was happening to me. You see, I had always felt that God did not speak to me and I had been forgotten. The Holy Spirit spoke and gave me my purpose in life. My purpose was to spread the word on how God can heal and deliver those who felt like they were all alone while dealing with cancer or any life changing experience. My purpose was to speak to other women, men and children, telling them, "YOU CAN GET THROUGH THIS!" I knew what they were experiencing; the feeling of abandonment and isolation. From that point on I knew that I had to write my life challenges and story of *Why God Chose Me*. I had to jot down what I experienced, what I felt and what I had gone through in my life.

14

Resting In His Arms

To prepare for surgery and to relax my mind, my parents, the kids and I went to Wisconsin Dells for the New Year celebration and declaration of a new beginning! We returned January 5, 2007 and surgery was scheduled four days later. For some reason, DaQuan was really frightened with this surgery. I guess maybe it was because of me having some previous complications and required returns to the hospital as experienced before that made him so apprehensive this time. He was there and saw me through all previous sicknesses, both physical and emotional. He just did not want to see me suffer any more. He seemed to cling to me the days before and just wanted to stay close as if he was protecting me from all hurt, harm or danger. I had to reassure him that if God got us through all that we had already gone through to date, there was no way that He was going to desert us now. I calmed him down and told him that everything would be okay.

So on January 9, 2007, I arrived at the hospital for surgery at 6:30 a.m. My Mom and aunt accompanied me to the hospital. Of course, my Dad did his usual duties of seeing my son off to school. Rev. Francine Stark was with my Mom in the waiting area of the hospital as she was during the first surgery. She has such a calming and reassuring spirit. She felt just like an angel that God has placed in my life. I was at peace with my life, my medical challenges and my life destiny and purpose. I knew in my heart and soul that I was going to be fine.

The combination of surgeries was to last about five to six hours. However, they lasted seven and a half hours instead. During surgery, I had to have two pints of blood administered. Coming out of surgery, true mature womanhood kicked in, I instantly went into menopause! I remained in the hospital for five days due to the fact that I needed an additional two more pints of blood. They also wanted to make sure that I did not have any blood clots or any other possible complications, especially with me being diabetic.

Everything was well, even though scarred, I now have two breast and no more periods. Further down the road, additional surgery will be required to make final adjustments with the completion of the left breast. This time looking in the mirror, I found myself realizing that the outer appearance no longer matters. I am stronger on the inside because of all that I had experienced. I am stronger because I know that God had been with me from the beginning to now. It no longer matters that my breast are smaller or that one is a little different from the other. It does not matter that I was bald or that my hair is short. What truly matters the most is that *I am alive*; *I am still here* and a *protected child of God*. I am here to talk about my struggles to help the next woman, man, boy or girl; to assist them with understanding why they are going through the challenges that they are facing. I am here to serve God as vessel and a witness of His power and ability to heal not only the body, but the soul. I want to let people know that yes, there will be times of sorrow and feelings of giving up. But YOU CAN NOT give up. You must persevere, you must endure, and you must go on! You will and can make it. Never let anyone tell you how you are suppose to feel, or let them tell you that it is okay and that you should not feel the way that you do. Honor your true feelings. Work through them when you are frustrated, angry or confused. They do not understand or will never be able to walk in *your* shoes. They do not know what you are going through or how sick you feel. They cannot fathom how tired you get sometimes and feel like giving up. How you have to smile to keep from crying or you have to cry when you cannot smile. No one can tell you how you are supposed to feel when you look at yourself and feel less than who you are. When you feel ugly rather than pretty, look deformed rather than normal—NO, they can not. But, please know that going through it all will empower you to go through with whatever life confronts you with. At whatever point, you have the ability to strive onward. The Lord will get you through it, if you allow Him to. He will give you peace and let you know that He has got your back. Put yourself in cruise control and be healed in Jesus' Name.

15

Accepting The Now

I am currently on long term disability and am suffering with continuous pain that radiates down my arm to my hand. With so many cancerous lymph nodes removed, there must have been some permanent nerve damage. I am also experiencing lymphedema, swelling in the left arm and hand. As a matter of fact, in order to produce this reflection of my life's purpose, I had to record my story on a voice recorder so that my Mom could type this book. I know now that God does things for a purpose, a season and a reason. But, as you go through, we must be able to follow the purpose, accept the season and discern the reason. No matter what the "it" is, whether it's cancer, a life struggle, a hardship or crisis, you can make it!! I am a living witness of this! I am here to tell you that there are times that you must share. You must speak to someone when you are feeling that you are at your lowest point. You must talk to someone who is going through, to someone who has gone through or even to someone who is about to go through. Talking and sharing will not only strengthen you but the other person as well. Most of all, it will also assist you in putting your "it" in perspective. It provides a sweet sense of prioritizing what really matters as well as who really matters in your life. We must learn to become our brother's keeper so that we can be available vessels for others, to assist and encourage them.

If we take a serious look back over our life, we will find that whatever we have gone through is nothing but a stepping stone of strength for the right-now situation. As I look back, I can see the empowerment that came from my molestation, troubled relationships, teenage pregnancy, dealing with the multiple surgeries, dealing with diabetes, and yes, even dealing with cancer. They were all faith exercises and push-ups for divine intervention. I thank God everyday for the blessing and rest in the fact that He will take care of it all—my health, my wealth and my peace. Matthew will be home soon and we will be able to live our lives as planned and discussed. We must keep God first in our life and in the plans that we make together.

Now, I know that it is my duty and commission to go out into the world to tell what the Lord has done for me; to speak of His goodness and mercy. To reassure others that what He has done for me, He can and will do for them as well. I am no longer afraid of expressing my feelings, emotions and sharing my survivor story. It is an awesome feeling to know what exactly my purpose is in life and be willing to walk in His predestined journey for me. I have begun my destiny by speaking at different schools, churches and functions about **Why God Chose Me**. I have shared my story and was featured in the Urban Spectrum newspaper out of Denver, Colorado on the topic of "Why Are So Many African American Women Dying of Breast Cancer?" I have also started my own support group called **P.I.N.K. (Passing Inspiration N Knowledge)**. The first session was a success and I give all praises to God for His vision that He put in me. **P.I.N.K.** is greatly needed; not just for family and friends, but for me as well. The continued healing, faith and strength is still a requirement.

Why Are So Many African-American Women Dying Of Breast Cancer?

By Christina Childrey

This year, the American Cancer Society estimates 19,010 African-American women will be diagnosed with breast cancer, and 5,000 will die from the disease. Research shows that African-American women are more likely than Caucasian women to be diagnosed at a younger age, have larger, more aggressive tumors, and to die of breast cancer.

Breast cancer is a disease that causes cells in the breast tissue to grow out of control and form a lump called a tumor. Most tumors are not cancerous; however, only a physician's examination can determine whether cancer exists.

The disease has four stages. When the disease is caught in its early stages, the survival rate is high and it's less likely that a woman will have to remove one or both breasts. A few of the many factors contributing to why Black women are less likely to survive this disease are late diagnosis, family history, lack of health insurance, obesity, poverty, clinical trials, and not being aware of new medical technology.

"When I first saw the doctor I was told the lump was related to my menstrual cycle. Six months later, I noticed a change in my breast. I did a self exam and noticed a lump. I thought about what the doctor said before, and I just brushed it off because I was near my menstrual cycle," said Monique Rhea of Chicago, a soon-to-be married mother of one.

In August, Rhea felt the lump again underneath her arm and within a couple days, "I couldn't lay on my stomach, my breast hurt really bad, and my skin felt like an orange peel," she said.

This time she went to a different doctor, thinking everything should be fine. On August 22, 2005, at the age of 32, she found out she had stage III breast cancer.

"I thought breast cancer was a disease that affected older white women. I've since chosen to have my left breast removed," Rhea explained.

In June 2006, another checkup found the cancer had spread to her lung, moving her into stage IV. This January, she had a hysterectomy. Soon, she will have breast reconstructive surgery.

"I've learned to be strong, and that just because you have breast cancer doesn't mean you have a death sentence," she said.

Like Rhea, African-American women are more likely to be diagnosed when the disease has progressed to its late stages, even though in her case, she followed the standard recommendations. She did a breast self exam once a month by checking for any changes in the shape, size, and texture of the breast, nipple, or areola (the ring of color around the nipple), and for any discharge, pain, lump, or thickening in the breast or under arm areas.

Dr. Jundel Allen-Davis, gynecologist and associate director of external relations at Kaiser Permanente of Colorado, advised you should never let the sun set on a breast lump, meaning if you notice one, don't leave it until tomorrow; get it examined right away.

Low participation in clinical trials can also be a disadvantage to African-American women, whose type of

Monique Rhea with fiance and son (below)

breast cancer is not responsive to certain treatments. The lack of African Americans in these trials leads to a lack of understanding in the medical field as to how a drug may respond differently in African Americans.

These trials allow doctors to find new ways to prevent, diagnose, treat, and possibly find cures for diseases. While doctors are less likely to talk to African Americans about clinical trials, some trials have strict guidelines that may exclude participants who have more than one disease such as diabetes and

"You should never let the sun set on a breast lump. If you notice one, don't leave it until tomorrow; get it examined right away."

Just when I thought my book was complete, on October 3, 2007, my Uncle LeVoyd (my Dad's oldest brother) died from pancreatic cancer. His suffering lasted for far too long, however, through it all, he remained faithful. To top things off, the next day, October 4, 2007, we found out that my Dad has prostate cancer. I was a little worried with how he would take the news and deal with now his struggles. However, I learned that my Dad used me as an example of showing strength, empowerment and faith. With his news, he said that while seeing me go through what I did and I still stood tall, he could get through anything.

Wait that is not the end of it, on October 15, 2007 I received a call from my doctor indicating that one of my cancer markers were elevated. And you know what was next, more testing needed. I was a little disappointed when hearing this at first because in July 2007, my cancer markers and PET Scan were normal and in August 2007, my mammogram was normal. After receiving the results, I was told that the right breast showed a mass and there was activity in my lymph nodes under the right armpit. The doctor suggested a mastectomy of the right breast and removal of the lymph nodes. Here we go again, more surgery. But I thank God that with today's technology, this was caught. Just think all this has happened within a few months time. I am not sure if chemotherapy or radiation is required, but I will continue to stand firm through it all.

In the interim, on October 31, 2007, we found out that my Aunt Martha (my Dad's second to youngest sister) has leukemia. Although it is evident that the devil is truly busy, I know that God is still real. I believe that all things happen for a reason and a season. Maybe God is allowing some things to happen and come to pass for our unity and strength. God is still in the midst of it all and He is still in control!!

So you see, even though you might be faced with many challenges, life threatening situations or circumstances beyond your control, you still have the ability to change your response to them. Your response might make your "going through" better, less challenging, and even more endurable. However, even though you are going through, as my Pastor, Dr. Rev. Alan V. Ragland once said in a sermon, you must remember that going through sometimes means "TH Rough". Life can get rough, but you can get rougher. Challenges may get hard, but you can get harder. Circumstances may get out of control, but you can be in control. Remember while you are going through, you must surround yourself with positive influences, positive people and keep a positive attitude. I had all of the above, a supporting man, supporting children, supporting parents, supporting siblings, supporting family and a supporting church. But most importantly, I have the love and support of God.

You can be a survivor in any situation, trial or tribulation. So today, I challenge you with passing the torch and passing this information to as many people that you know. We can no longer be silent and be afraid to express our feelings and our own survivor stories. May God continue to bless you and be with you as He is continually with me!!!

Reflections from My Family & Friends

We know that breast cancer as well as any disease, not only affects the person afflicted, but also family and friends too. The following are reflections of those dear to me.

Reflection from my soul mate, Matthew O. Dilworth

To my Bae,

First, I give praises to God for blessing our family. I would like to thank God for giving Monique another life. Bae, you know that I love you with all my heart and there are not enough words to express the deep love I have for you. You are a beautiful and caring woman. This is one of the reasons why I love you so much. I love you for YOU and for who you are—that will never change no matter what may come.

Bae, this has truly been a rough journey for us both but with God, we have made it! When you love someone so much, it is hard to accept when something is wrong with them. I have been in the situation of having a love one with cancer and Lord knows that I never wanted another loved one to go through the same thing. It is very hard on me and there are truly no words to say how I feel. Because no one would ever like to see a loved one go through pain or ups and downs. What really hurt me the most was that I could not be there for my mother, Ora Dilworth as well as for the woman that I love, Monique L Rhea.

In view of the fact that I was unable to be with Mama or by your side, I felt that I was not really supportive enough of either of you. Nothing could help, no matter what I said or try to do; it just never felt that it was good enough or suitable. I knew that I needed to be by your side, day in and day out. To comfort you, to be there for you, to share with you in all of your struggles—but, I could not. The only support that I could give was through pen and paper. Or through the calls that were made, but to me, that was never good enough.

When you told me that my beautiful woman had breast cancer, I did not know how to accept those words. I did not want them to be said or to be true. I was very much afraid because I did not know what to expect or what the outcome would be. I did not even want the thought of losing you to cross my mind. So I stayed positive and kept praying to God. GOD ANSWERED ALL OF OUR PRAYERS. Now I am blessed because your surgeries have gone well and you are okay. This was the most important thing to us all. I pray that things will only get better from this point on. Monique, I love you with all my heart, mind, and soul. Words can never express how much I love you, Baby.

Love You,
Matt

Reflections from my Mom, Terri V. Rhea

My Dearest Daughter, Monique,

Thank God for you and for the blessed privilege and opportunity of trying to provide some reflections during our journey through some of our life challenges over the past eighteen months. I am very proud of you and I thank you for the honor of being included in your testimony. Yes, it has truly been an experience these past few months of which I do not think either of us can or will forget. I can still hear the urgency in your voice on that day in August of 2005. Your Dad and I were just two days into a well needed vacation at a timeshare presentation, hundreds of miles away in Puerto Vallarta. The time was truly needed as the family had been going through some life adjustments beginning June 2004:

~ Mama said, "Yes" to Heaven's gates on June 29, 2004

~ Mama's close friend, Gussie, joined Mama 3 months later, September, 2004

~ 2nd mom, Mama Rhea (Dallas Rhea), grew very weak, became bed-ridden

~ Brother, Michael, said "Yes" to Heaven in July, 2005

~ Brother, Donnie, was sickly

As I remember your call, I can still hear the message ringing in my ears. I could hear your voice but exactly what you were saying and the impact of it all, was not registering. I guess I was in a state of shock. You had an x-ray and biopsy previous to our departure and were awaiting the outcome the following week that we were to be away. I can hear your voice as clear as if it was happening today. What did she just say? How do I respond? We were so many miles away! Do I leave vacation to get back to my child? What should I do, what true words can reassure her with us so far away? Oh, if I could only hug and kiss away the fear and uncertainty as Moms do when their child gets hurt. But this was one hurt my kiss could not ease nor remove. I sat there dumfounded; I guess my face was reflecting the horror of it all to those who around me as I was asked what as wrong. My eyes became glassy and I am sure that I must have had a blank look on my face, again, they asked, "What's wrong?"

As I looked at Louis, I could see in his eyes that he knew what I was about to say. How do I say this, how can the news be given without hurting so much. I knew there was no real way of giving news like this, I just lower the phone, took a deep breath and said in a soft voice stated, "It's cancerous." The circle of friends and family shed tears as we just sat there in silence for a few seconds. Then your Dad and I were given words of comfort and encouragement as a close family and friends would do. To be honest, I can only guess what the words were as it is still all a blurb to me. What are the only words anyone could say in a situation like this, "It's going to be okay." "The Lord will take care of her." "She's strong, everything will be alright." You know as I am writing these words now, they seem so shallow and empty. But, knowing from whom the words were coming from, I know they were given in belief and sincerity.

You said that you would be okay and requested that we finish our vacation. I have to take this opportunity to write how much I appreciate your *girls* who came to your side in our absence. After their call, in a matter of minutes, they surrounded you, they kept you comforted and attended to you for the rest of the week. Thank

God for family at times of trouble and challenges. I am reminded of scripture in I Corinthians, Chapter 12:25-26:

> *This makes for harmony among the members; so that all the members care for each other equally. If one part suffers, all the parts suffer with it....*

Thanks for being there for your family and my first-born. You will never know how the rest of the week enabled me to become strengthen for the journey ahead. The journey that proved that I was required to utilize all the spiritual tools that I had learned, believed, and trusted about the Lord. In my heart of heart, I truly knew that He in fact was alive, true to His Word and that He would be there when I call upon Him. It was up to me to be the initiator and activator to the "line of communication". I braced myself for the journey and rested in God's arms. I must admit that there were days that were harder than others. I felt I had to be the "rock" for you, for DaQuan and for your Dad. But to be honest, there were times that I felt as if I was in quicksand, that I was being pulled down into a pit. It was like the more I struggled to be everyone's all, I became my nothing. One time my nothingness was pretty evident was when I had a private breakdown. I began to ask God, "Why me? Why my daughter, can't this pass? Won't You please let this cup pass us by? Why? Why? Why, I kept asking. My mind ran over all the family trials and challenges over the months that we were experiencing. To say the least, I guess I officially had my own pity party.

I sat there a few seconds and it was like a calmness came over me and an instant response was given. "I know what you are feeling. I know how it is to love your child as a parent. I too can relate because I know how I felt as I watched my Child suffer too". From that point on, I chose to rely on the Lord and to get a grip on myself. I chose not to let anyone or anything make me doubt nor shake my foundation. I knew that I must start believing and relying on the Lord for all I needed. The Book of Psalms became a resting place for me. The Holy Spirit would randomly lead me to a selection on which I would meditate. Close friends and church organizations would call, send cards and give inspirational books and emails to both you and me. Thru these inspirational touches, I was able to stand and believe, sit and listen, let go and allow, pray and rest.

I thank God for using His vessels to give special nuggets like those given at just the right time to both you and me. No matter how spiritual or grounded one may think that they are, there may come a time that a situation or circumstance will shake your very foundation. If we are not careful, we can allow our spiritual foundation to become cracked, allowing the infiltration of doubt and loss of hope. Or if not spiritually sealed, the crack will cause the leakage of all that we know to be true and solid.

Yes, we have had some rough trials. Yes, we have asked the whys, what's next and the how come. But, along this journey and through it all, I have seen your growth. You are becoming a strong pillar not only for the Lord, yourself and your son, but an inspiration to others that are also being challenged by life experiences. So continue on as life is opening herself to you and if by chance your foundation becomes a little weak or even become cracked, and you begin to ask, "Why God chose me?" Just remember the words from John, Chapter 15, verse 16(NLT):

> *You did not choose me, I chose you. I appointed you to go and produce fruit that will last, so that the Father will give you whatever you ask for, using my name.*

So, my Dearest Daughter, be confident, be strong and BE CHOSEN.

Love Mom

Reflections from my father, John L. Rhea

From your one and only Diddy,

I was devastated and hurt because I could not be there for you when you initially heard the news. You never know how cancer can affect you until you are hit with it yourself. I always asked why as well. I cried and hurt just as much as you did. I even called my sister several times to pray for me as well as Terri, I was going through. It really had gotten rough and I wanted to make sure that I could continue to be strong for us all.

I have always been a joking type of person. I guess this is why I joked all the time during your days of baldness and the lost of your breast. I knew laughter would help you along the way. But through it all, we made it this far and will continue to do so.

Love you,
Dad

Reflections from my son, DaQuan T. Dilworth (fourteen years old)

Dear Mom,

How did I feel when I found out that you had cancer? I did not know what was going on. I was really scared and mad because I really cared about you a lot and I love you so much. I was not doing good in school because I was worried about you. I was getting frustrated a lot. I use to check on you all the time to make sure you were not dead and to also make sure your blood sugar was straight. I wanted you to stay alive and stay healthy.

I thank God that you are still here because without you I would not be here. I have to be thankful because some kids do not have a Mom or Dad because they were taking drugs or have died from different types of cancer. But God kept you here for a reason and I thank Him for that.

Love you Mom,
DaQuan

Reflections from my daughter, Meia M. Brown (fifteen years old)

Dear Monique,

How did I feel when I found out that you had Breast Cancer? I was sad, angry, worried and I just did not know what to think at that point. I do not think you or anyone else deserves to be in a situation like you were in. I know you are blessed because you are still here with us. You are still happy, beautiful and loving.

Everyone who is reading this book should know that you are a very caring person and fun to be around. And I must also mention a gorgeous person. When you lost your hair and one breast, it did not change the way I felt about you and it should be the same for anyone else. I think with hair or no hair both breast or no breast you are still beautiful inside and outside. I just want to let you know that I loved you before this situation ever came about and I still love you now, but even more. I appreciate everything your family and you have ever done for me.

Love you,
Meia

Reflections from my daughter, Miesha L. Brown
(thirteen years old)

Dear Monique,

When I found out that you had breast cancer, I felt very sad. I felt sad because I did not know if you were going to survive or die. But I was hoping and praying that you would survive. You were doing well and then one day I found out that the cancer had come back, but this time in your lungs.

I was thinking to myself, "She was doing good. Why did the cancer come back?" I became scared again because I knew that you would have to fight again and again to beat the cancer. Then when I found out that you were cancer free, I was very happy because I do not know what I would do if you had died.

Love you,
Miesha

Reflections from brother, Renell L. Rhea

Dear Mo,

Let me start by saying that two things I feel are taken for granted are life and love. You should live life to the fullest because tomorrow is never guaranteed. The one you love may not always be there in your life, so while you live, tell the ones you have, you love them.

I was more in shock about hearing that my sister was diagnosed with cancer and was much worried. It was not suppose to happen, but we can not predict what situations God willed or has placed in our path of life. But it is never more than what we can bare. I knew because of faith, prayer and your strength that you would prevail over anything. I love you Mo and I am always here for you.

Love you,
Renell

Reflections from sister, Ottawa C. Rhea

Dear Sister …

I Don't Know If You Knew….

I don't know if you knew … the more I tried to reject the sister-hood relationship, the more I knew it would come to pass. I could not run from it any longer; it was in my face and in the presence of my life daily. You were someone whom I had grown to love.

I don't know if you knew … I was there physically when you were told that you had cancer, but emotionally I was absent. As crazy as it may sound, with other family members surrounding you, I did not want to feel the possibility of a rejection or to go unnoticed as I was accustomed to in my past. The day they wheeled you in your hospital room, I sat in shock waiting on my turn to see my sister.

I don't know if you knew … Because of some failed challenges and fears from my past, I did not want to lose you also. How do you fight something inside of someone being afflicted and still love the suffering person? I kept telling myself that I will not let this take you from me. I will not be rejected by a word called "Cancer". I asked, why God would let this happen to you. It was not until I realized that it happened to you so that you could understand your purpose in life.

I don't know if you knew … Momma said the day I married your brother that she always wanted twins. As much as we hate to admit it, we are alike in many ways. Twins share a bond that no one or anything can come between, not even cancer.

I don't know if you knew … I love you Sister and thank God everyday for your life. As twins, we feel the same things. So when you hurt, I hurt. When you are happy, I am happy with you.

I don't know if you knew … but I cried my last tear yesterday.

Love your Twin for life,
Ottawa

Reflections from my brother, Myron Dilworth

A heavy heart full of hurt and pain that words can not describe. If someone in your life whom you loved dearly was going through a process and you were not able to assist them then, you know the hurt and pain I speak of.

I was afraid that this special someone's work here on earth was done and scared that God was ready to add her to his kingdom. I was fighting the temptation of fear and was confused as to why God would allow an illness to visit another someone that I loved.

I gained control of my faith and believed that everything would be fine because I knew Who was in control. I prayed to God that He would take my life instead of hers if her destiny was to be ended.

This special someone I speak of is Monique L. Rhea! With love and appreciation, I am grateful to have a sister with her helpfulness, insight and caring support. I love you sister more than words can express … Monique L. Rhea, I love you dearly.

Love always,
Your Little Bro, Myron

Reflections from my Lil Sis, Melanie L. Ragland

I grew up an only child, and although I had a big extended family and plenty of friends, I used to wonder what it would be like to have a big sister. As I got older, I just adopted my sisters and they adopted me. I was probably around 13 or 14 years old when I first started getting close to Monique. She was one of my Girl Scout leaders, of which our group had a lot of fun together. Over the years as I went through high school, Monique joined my roster of big sisters, and she has continued to do many big sister things for me. Countless times, she has talked to me, given me advice, and given me rides to and from the airport when I was coming in and out of town. Monique has even fed me and taught me how to balance a check book! Like a big sister, she gets upset and yells at me when I do stupid things. One time, she told me, "Do not ever do that again, Mel! I can not even talk about this anymore. You made my blood sugar go up!" She was serious, but I could not help but to laugh. My sister Monique has always made herself available to me, and has been with me in some of the best and worst times I have ever had.

When Monique told me that she had breast cancer, I remember thinking that it was my turn to be there for her, but, how in the world would I do that? What should I say? She was always the one telling me what to do! And, I worried that I was not saying or doing the right things to make it easier for her, like I wanted to. Monique talked to me about the physical changes she was going through, and I could not imagine what it would be like to experience that, especially since she had already had some other health challenges. I was afraid for her. But, Monique did not feel sorry for herself too long. As a matter of fact, she continued to encourage herself and others, even if it was sent by way of an inspirational email every now and then (which I *did* read, by the way, Monique!). I was so impressed with the courage she showed. Before breast cancer, she had been an example to me. Now, she is an example to the world. I am so proud of her for writing this book and sharing her experiences.

God is in control, and our bodies belong to Him. Monique has come through breast cancer victoriously. I look back and am thankful for the faith that she had all along and for the faith that others had to pray for her. I am thankful that God saw fit to deliver her from cancer and to use her to help others. Most of all, I am glad that Monique knows that she is a walking miracle of God. She knows that God—not her doctors, radiation, and chemotherapy—is the reason she is alive, and she wants everybody else to know this same thing.

God bless your work, Monique

Love you,
Mel

Reflections from my nephew, Christopher L. Dilworth (fifteen years old)

Dear Auntie,

As I think back on my reflections and reactions of when I found out you had breast cancer, I wanted to cry. I had a lot of thoughts running through my mind. Some of the thoughts that ran across my mind were "Is she going to die or will she survive? What will happen next?" These thoughts came to my mind because the people I experienced with cancer died, got really sick or were unable to continue on with their daily lives.

I wanted to spend as much time as I could with you because I did not know if this would be the time that you would leave this earth for good. Even though I did not act like it sometimes, this is how I truly felt. I love you with all my heart and I do not want anything to keep you from your family and friends. My tears of sadness eventually turned into tears of joy. The reason I say tears of joy instead of tears of sadness is because after all the stuff you went through, you are still here and survived it all.

Love you,
Chris

Reflections from my niece, RaNiya C. Rhea
(seven years old)

To Tee-Tee

When I found out my Tee-Tee had breast cancer, I felt kind of sad because she had to leave the house a lot to get chemo. I was worried about her because I thought that she would get really really sick and die. I did not like that she had to get a lot of shots for her boom boom (breast). She was so sick when I would come over, she could not play and do a lot of stuff with me. It would be hard to be around all the other family and my Tee-Tee was not around. I wanted her all to myself when she got home but there was a lot of people around her. I really did not like when I could not see her at the hospital because I was too young to get in. I thought I would never see her again. But now I am really happy because she is always home and now we can play again. I love you Tee-Tee and I am glad that you are better. But I hate cancer because it almost took you away from me.

Love you,
Stink (Tee-Tee Baby)

Reflections from my Uncle Bomb, "Uncle Bobble Head"
Keith Talley

Nique,

First of all, I would like to thank you for entrusting me with the privilege of proof reading your work of art "***Why God Chose Me***". You are truly and amazing woman, because through it all you stayed positive, steadfast, strong and resilient enough to put all your thoughts, feelings and tribulations into words. Most of us could not even start a book, including me, let alone complete a book in such a short period of time.

Secondly, I must thank your parents, my sister and brother, for instilling all the values, such as faith, trust, and love, in your heart, for the Creator. For God has blessed you with decidedness and wisdom to know your purpose in this world. He has brought you this far and will take you even further in future endeavors.

Thirdly, I would like to thank you for welcoming Kevin and I into the family the way you did. You were the first one to call me "Uncle" and you took Kevin under your wing and helped him through the difficult time he had after losing his mother. He followed you around all the time up until the time you helped teach him how to drive, and then you were just another adult just like Donna and I were. It is funny, that you and I were always competing against each other because I think we are very much alike in certain ways. (I'm gonna check your D.N.A. cause I believe you are my niece, not your Aunt Donna's) Little did you know that you exhibited guidance and nurturing to my son that set the table for you becoming a great mother to DaQuan.

With all that being said, I really enjoyed "***Why God Chose Me***", it was very well written, had some surprising twists, was very informative and even though I cried through some portions, I am very happy to know that "**YOU ARE A SURVIVOR**"!

P.S.… You are pretty in P.I.N.K.!!!!

Love, kisses and hugs,
Uncle Bomb
Keith D. Talley

Reflections from my Girls Cousins

~*Kimberly A. McLendon*

During this time of trials and tribulations, I was scared and at a lost. Instead I gained a sister, a best friend. You are my Survivor. You are a Blessing. You are my Angel.

Love Ya, Kim

~*Candace L. Boyd*

I cried for several days, afraid that you were going to die because of the lost of past family members dying of cancer. My biggest fear was I was not strong enough for you. I wanted you to know that you could always fall on me for support. I thought I was going to lose my best friend, but through praying, we made it!!

Love you Boo, Candy

~*Dionne M. Rutherford*

The "Big Day",

The day Monique found out that she had cancer, she called we ran. After that run, we ran to Cold Stone (comfort food). I watched how she went thru radiation and chemo, and how it took a toll over her body not once but twice. But each time she made it. My prayer for Monique is that she stands tall and listens to the sweet whisper of God's voice.

Love, Dionne

~*Erica D. Bolden*

When I heard that you had breast cancer, I was hurt. I kept saying "This was not supposed to happen. She is the baby of the bunch". I would not wish this on anyone. But I am glad that you are feeling better.

Love you cuz, Erica

~Andrea L. Moore

Initially when I found out about Monique's diagnosis of breast cancer I sat in my car and cried like a baby. I was thinking, "Not my cousin!!!! She is not old enough for this!!!!!!!" During the ordeal I prayed constantly for God to heal her and allow this trial to become her ministry. A ministry that she can use to reach other young African American women who think they are all alone during this time. I also wanted to be there for her as much as possible. Despite my hectic schedule, I had the opportunity of taking her for a round of chemotherapy. Watching Monique press through this trial has allowed me to be a witness to a stronger side never before seen. God's healing power is no joke and is so real. Despite the battle, I thank God for the victory of healing in my cousin's life. And I look forward to the places that God will take her in ministry.

Love you, Andi

Reflections from my oldest godchild, MonCheri' L. McLendon

Dear Monique,

All of the events in my life have happened for a reason. The most powerful event that has happened so far is finding out that you were diagnosed with breast cancer. At first, I felt that this was not possible but then I saw that it was. I did not know how to react because someone that close to me had never been this sick or going through what you went through. You are a true survivor and you are a gift from God.

I feel that this has brought us closer together and made me not take life for granted. I am glad that you came into my life and made a good impression on me. Bad can happen to the best of us, but only the strongest can survive it. It hurt that it had to happen to you. Nothing in life is guaranteed and everyone should feel blessed that they are still lucky to even still be living and even living healthy.

Love you,
Lil Me to Big Me

Reflections from a true friend/cousin, LaToya Jones

Dear Monique,

When I received the call from you stating that you had breast cancer, I tried to stay strong while on the phone with you. Once we hung up, I immediately started to sob. I could not believe that this was happening to you. I felt that we are too young to experience such trauma. Right today, I am still too afraid to give myself breast exams. I felt that you were so strong and smart to discover your own lumps.

This is a ridiculous statement, but I felt that if I had been in your life as much as I use to be, this might not have occurred. I instantly felt that it was time for me to step up and get back involved in my friend/cousin's life and help out as much as I could. I always mentioned in the back of my mind that if you left this earth and I was not there, I would feel horrible. I had not spent as much time with you as I should have and could have. At that moment, I wanted back the years that we missed with each other so that I could have more time with you. I wanted back the relationship, the laughter, the tears, the arguments, the walks and talks to school, the intimate secrets we shared, the overall closeness, etc … Instantaneously, I stop feeling sorry for you and decided to show the support you needed. I can not go back in time, but it is not too late to go forward and rebuild our relationship. Overall the disease showed me how much I missed you.

Love you,
Toy

Reflections from a true friend, Cynthia Brown

I remember the day Monique told me that she felt a lump in her breast. It was a Monday, I know because we rode to work together on Mondays. So I assured her that it was nothing to worry about, but that she should get it checked out just to be sure. I never imagined that a person's life could change so drastically in such a short period of time. Within two weeks, Monique had found a lump and learned that she had breast cancer. I cried that day because I did not know how or what I could do for a friend who had done so much for me. But the worst was not over.

As I look back, I think that no one expected, or would have wished, for Monique to experience such a horrible thing. However, I thank God for her because through her trials we all have grown stronger. It was this disease that made everyone around her thankful for the little things. It was because of this disease that the bonds of friendship and family were strengthening in her life and mine. It was this situation that made even my mother just a little closer to me because she saw the pain I was going through. Monique's story is not just her story, it became *our* story. I love her for the intentional kindness she has shown me and for the things she gave me without even knowing.

Cynthia

978-0-595-47966-5
0-595-47966-9